EMPOWERING UTILITIES

The Strategic Role of Product Owners

Zachary Beaty MBA, PMP

ISBN: 9798877667662

Imprint: Independently published
Cover design by: Art Painter
Printed in the United States of America

CONTENTS

INTRODUCTION

◆ ◆ ◆

In the dynamic landscape of the utility industry, where challenges and opportunities converge, the role of a Product Owner emerges as a strategic linchpin for innovation and progress. As the demand for reliable and sustainable utility services grows, so does the need for professionals who can navigate the intricate intersection of technology, regulations, and market dynamics.

"Empowering Utilities: The Strategic Role of Product Owners" embarks on a comprehensive exploration of this pivotal profession, offering insights into the evolution of the utility sector and the crucial role product owners play in driving transformative change. Within these pages, you will dive into the nuances of strategic product ownership, emphasizing the collaborative leadership required to navigate the complexities of an industry shaped by regulation, technological advancements, and shifting consumer expectations.

As you embark on this journey, keep in mind the aim is to equip both seasoned professionals and aspiring product owners with the knowledge, skills, and strategic vision necessary to navigate the unique challenges of the utility sector. By understanding the intricacies of stakeholder dynamics, embracing agile methodologies, and weaving together success stories and best practices, this book serves as a high level guide for those committed to shaping the future of utilities through effective product ownership.

Join in unraveling the layers of the utility industry, where innovation meets necessity, and discover how product owners can be catalysts for transformative growth and sustainability.

PART I: NAVIGATING THE COMPLEX TERRAIN OF THE UTILITY LANDSCAPE INDUSTRY DYNAMICS

REGULATORY FRAMEWORK: UNRAVELING THE LEGAL TAPESTRY

◆ ◆ ◆

The historical evolution of regulations in the electric utility industry has played a pivotal role in shaping both the industry's structure and the trajectory of product development. During the late 19th and early 20th centuries, as power generation and distribution systems emerged, the industry operated with minimal regulations. However, concerns about potential monopolistic abuses prompted the establishment of regulatory frameworks, with public utility commissions overseeing state-level rates, service standards, and utility investments.

In the mid-20th century, a regulatory and monopolistic phase unfolded, where exclusive franchises were granted to ensure fair rates and universal service. This regulatory environment significantly influenced the type of products developed within the industry, emphasizing compliance with regulated standards and ensuring equitable access.

The later 20th century witnessed a paradigm shift towards deregulation and restructuring, separating functions to introduce competition and reduce costs. This transformation not only reshaped the industry landscape but also influenced product development, with a heightened focus on innovation to gain a competitive edge in emerging markets.

Simultaneously, the growing prominence of environmental concerns led to regulations promoting renewable energy adoption and energy efficiency. These regulatory initiatives directly impacted the development of products within the electric utility sector, driving innovation toward cleaner and more sustainable technologies.

In the 21st century, regulatory focus extended to technological advancements like smart grids and energy storage, aiming to enhance grid reliability and flexibility. These regulations not only paved the way for the adoption of cutting-edge technologies but also steered research and development efforts within the industry.

Ongoing regulatory trends continue to address emerging challenges, highlighting the dynamic interplay between regulations and product development in the electric utility sector. As the industry progresses, regulatory frameworks are likely to remain a driving force behind innovative product development, particularly in response to evolving environmental, technological, and market dynamics.

Product owners in the electric utility industry face a complex environment characterized by both regulatory constraints and opportunities. Compliance with local, state, and federal regulations is paramount, encompassing safety standards, environmental requirements, and industry-specific mandates. Non-compliance can result in penalties and damage to a company's reputation. Standardization and interoperability regulations, set by regulatory bodies, create consistency but may limit product flexibility. Rate regulation overseen by regulatory bodies can constrain pricing strategies, ensuring fairness for consumers but potentially impacting revenue generation. The push for cleaner energy has introduced stringent environmental regulations, necessitating products that adhere to emissions standards and energy efficiency guidelines. Cybersecurity and data privacy regulations are crucial, given the increasing digitization of the industry.

On the flip side, regulatory opportunities exist for product owners. Incentive programs and environmental credits encourage the development of innovative and sustainable technologies. Market expansion opportunities may arise from regulatory changes, such as the liberalization of energy markets.

Environmental and renewable energy credits provide additional incentives. Innovation and research funding can be accessed by aligning projects with regulatory goals, and strategic partnerships with regulatory bodies and industry stakeholders offer valuable insights and potential collaboration opportunities. In navigating this intricate regulatory landscape, staying informed, adapting to changes, and strategically leveraging opportunities are critical for success in product development within the electric utility sector.

MARKET TRENDS AND EMERGING TECHNOLOGIES: PIONEERING THE FUTURE

As technology continues to advance and consumer expectations evolve, staying abreast of market trends and emerging technologies becomes paramount. From the rise of decentralized energy systems to the integration of Artificial Intelligence, the following explores how product owners can leverage emerging technologies such as smart grids, renewable energy sources, and advanced analytics to craft strategic product development initiatives that align with industry trends.

One prominent trend is the ascent of decentralized energy systems, representing a paradigm shift from traditional centralized power generation. This decentralization is fueled by the growing adoption of distributed energy resources (DERs) such as solar panels and energy storage solutions. Understanding and harnessing the potential of decentralized systems become crucial for product owners seeking to align their offerings with the evolving industry landscape.

Another focal point is the integration of Artificial Intelligence (AI) into the electric utility sector. AI technologies, including machine learning and predictive analytics, are empowering utilities to optimize operations, enhance grid management, and improve overall system efficiency.

Within this dynamic landscape, product owners are encouraged to navigate the intersection of market trends and emerging technologies. By understanding the implications of decentralized energy systems, integrating AI intelligently, and strategically leveraging technologies like smart grids, renewable energy sources, and advanced analytics, product owners can craft initiatives that not only meet consumer expectations but also position their offerings as catalysts for positive change in the sector.

STAKEHOLDER ANALYSIS: NURTURING COLLABORATIVE RELATIONSHIPS

The utility industry is a web of interconnected stakeholders, each with distinct interests, concerns, and roles. Effective product ownership hinges on the ability to navigate these intricate relationships. This section delves into the art of stakeholder analysis, offering a comprehensive guide on identifying, understanding, and collaborating with the diverse groups that influence product development within the utility sector.

In the journey of effective product ownership within the utility industry, the first crucial step involves mapping the intricate stakeholder landscape. Internally, this entails recognizing the pivotal roles played by engineering teams, regulatory compliance experts, and project managers, each contributing unique skills and perspectives to the product development process. Externally, the scope broadens to encompass diverse groups such as end-users, utility consumers, government regulators, environmental agencies, and industry associations. Understanding the distinct roles these external stakeholders play is essential for shaping the utility landscape.

The second key aspect involves delving into a nuanced understanding of stakeholder interests. Prioritizing the needs and expectations of end-users and utility consumers is paramount, urging product owners to conduct surveys, interviews, and usability studies to glean insights into preferences and pain points. Simultaneously, recognizing the significance of compliance with regulatory bodies becomes pivotal.

Understanding the specific regulations that impact product development and ensuring alignment with legal requirements are critical components of this stage.

Cultural and demographic considerations take center stage as the third element in effective stakeholder analysis. Acknowledging and analyzing the diversity within both internal and external stakeholders become imperative. Product owners need to consider how cultural and demographic factors may influence perceptions, preferences, and the adoption of utility products.

The fourth dimension revolves around creating collaborative structures that foster inclusivity throughout the product development lifecycle. Establishing cross-functional teams that bring together individuals from diverse departments is crucial for fostering collaboration and ensuring that all perspectives are considered. Additionally, forming advisory boards comprising representatives from different stakeholder groups allows ongoing consultation and input from key players in the utility sector.

Effective communication strategies form the fifth component, emphasizing the need to recognize that different stakeholders may require varied communication approaches. Tailoring messaging to address the specific concerns and interests of each group is essential. Transparency is a cornerstone, fostering a culture of openness in communications and clearly articulating the goals, progress, and potential impacts of the product development process to build trust among stakeholders.

The final stage involves incorporating stakeholder feedback, utilizing robust mechanisms to capture insights at various product development stages. This ensures continuous alignment with stakeholder expectations and needs. Embracing an iterative development approach that allows for adjustments based on ongoing stakeholder feedback becomes paramount. Navigating the intricate web of stakeholders within the utility industry is not just a skill; it is a strategic imperative for innovation and sustained success in product ownership. By meticulously mapping the stakeholder landscape, understanding their interests, and creating collaborative structures with effective communication, product owners can drive successful and inclusive product development initiatives.

BUILDING EFFECTIVE COMMUNICATION CHANNELS: FOSTERING TRANSPARENCY AND COLLABORATION

Communication is the backbone of successful product ownership. In the digital age, technology is a crucial driver of enhanced communication in product development. Product owners can capitalize on innovative tools and platforms to facilitate real-time information sharing and streamline collaboration. Utilizing project management software like Asana or Jira enables efficient project tracking, task assignment, and seamless collaboration. Communication platforms such as Slack or Microsoft Teams provide instant messaging and virtual meeting capabilities, fostering smooth team communication. Additionally, data analytics tools like Tableau empower product owners to extract valuable insights from data, contributing to strategic decision-making. Moving beyond digital platforms, the orchestration of stakeholder meetings becomes pivotal for effective communication. Regular and well-structured meetings serve as dynamic forums for exchanging ideas, addressing concerns, and fostering alignment in product development. Virtual meeting tools like Zoom or Microsoft Teams facilitate face-to-face interactions, even in remote work settings. Collaborative online whiteboards, such as Miro or MURAL, enhance visual communication during these meetings, allowing stakeholders to actively participate and contribute ideas. To navigate the complexity of the utility industry, product owners must possess a comprehensive understanding of industry dynamics and conduct thorough stakeholder analysis as already discussed. Tools like StakeholderMap or Lucidchart prove invaluable for visualizing stakeholder relationships, ensuring a nuanced understanding of their roles and interests. Effective communication emerges not merely as a tool but as a strategic imperative for successful product ownership in the utility industry. The strategic combination of leveraging technology, orchestrating stakeholder meetings, and understanding industry dynamics forms a solid foundation for subsequent chapters. Equipped with insights and practical strategies, product owners are well-positioned to steer their initiatives toward success in this dynamic landscape.

PART II: THE STRATEGIC PRODUCT OWNER

STRATEGIC VISION: NAVIGATING LONG-TERM SUCCESS

In the utility industry, especially within the realm of electric utilities, the significance of long-term planning cannot be overstated. As the demand for reliable and sustainable energy solutions continues to grow, product owners in this sector face the imperative of possessing a strategic vision that seamlessly aligns with the broader objectives of the organization. This strategic vision not only serves as a roadmap for the development of innovative products but also plays a pivotal role in navigating the complex and dynamic landscape of the electric utility sector.

Long-term planning in the utility industry involves anticipating and adapting to a myriad of factors, including technological advancements, regulatory changes, and shifts in consumer preferences. Product owners must exhibit foresight in understanding how these factors will shape the future of the electric utility sector and, consequently, the trajectory of their product development initiatives. This foresight is essential for ensuring that products are not only relevant and cutting-edge at the time of launch but also capable of withstanding the test of time.

Strategic vision in the electric utility sector extends beyond immediate market trends. It involves a holistic understanding of the industry's evolution towards cleaner and more sustainable energy solutions. This includes staying abreast of advancements in renewable energy technologies, energy storage systems, and smart grid infrastructure. A forward-thinking product owner in the electric utility sector recognizes the importance of aligning product development efforts with the global transition towards a more sustainable and environmentally friendly energy landscape.

Furthermore, the strategic vision of a product owner in the electric utility industry encompasses a proactive approach to regulatory dynamics. Given the heavily regulated nature of the sector, product owners need to anticipate and respond to changes in energy policies, environmental regulations, and grid management standards. Aligning product development strategies with regulatory goals ensures that new offerings not only comply with current standards but also position the organization to thrive amidst future regulatory shifts.

In addition to technological and regulatory considerations, a strategic vision for product owners in the electric utility sector involves understanding the diverse needs of stakeholders. This includes not only end-users but also utility operators, government agencies, and environmental organizations. Successful long-term planning requires a deep appreciation for the intricate web of relationships and interests within the industry, ensuring that products are developed to meet the expectations and requirements of a diverse array of stakeholders.

In the electric utility sector, where long-term planning is a cornerstone of success, product owners must embody a strategic vision that extends beyond immediate market conditions. This vision encompasses a thorough understanding of technological trends, regulatory landscapes, and stakeholder dynamics. By aligning their product development initiatives with broader organizational objectives and industry evolution, product owners can navigate the complexities of the electric utility sector and contribute meaningfully to its sustainable and innovative future.

ALIGNING PRODUCT GOALS WITH COMPANY OBJECTIVES

Key Performance Indicators (KPIs) and performance metrics serve as measurable indicators of progress toward product objectives. Product owners should establish clear connections between the KPIs relevant to their products and the broader strategic goals of the organization. This ensures that product success is not only defined by individual features but also by their contribution to overarching business outcomes.

An effective strategy for linking product development with

organizational objectives lies in the meticulous crafting of product roadmaps. Product owners should align their roadmaps with the strategic goals of the organization, ensuring that each product initiative contributes meaningfully to the overarching vision. By mapping out features, functionalities, and release timelines in tandem with organizational milestones, product roadmaps become a dynamic tool for translating strategic intent into tangible product outcomes.

In essence, the critical link between product development and organizational objectives is nurtured through a combination of strategic insight, collaboration, adaptability, and transparent communication. Product owners, as stewards of innovation, play a central role in weaving this connection seamlessly, ensuring that every product conceived and developed contributes effectively to the realization of the company's overarching mission, vision, and strategic aspirations.

ROADMAPPING: NAVIGATING SHORT-TERM AND LONG-TERM PRIORITIES

T he utility industry demands a delicate balance between addressing immediate needs and planning for the future. Product owners need a comprehensive understanding of the utility industry, encompassing current challenges, emerging trends, and long-term visions. This involves staying abreast of technological advancements, regulatory shifts, and market dynamics. A holistic view enables product owners to identify immediate pain points while anticipating future needs.

Engaging with a diverse array of stakeholders, including utility operators, regulators, and end-users, is essential. Stakeholder collaboration provides insights into immediate requirements and helps identify future trends. Regular communication ensures that roadmaps align with the evolving needs of the industry and its stakeholders.

Product owners must prioritize initiatives based on their impact on both immediate challenges and long-term goals. This involves assessing the urgency of addressing current issues while considering how each product development effort contributes to the strategic roadmap for the future. Prioritization ensures that resources are allocated judiciously.

Given the dynamic nature of the utility industry, roadmapping should be flexible and iterative. Product owners should embrace an agile approach, allowing for adjustments based on emerging trends, regulatory changes, and stakeholder feedback. Iterative planning ensures that roadmaps remain adaptable to evolving industry landscapes.

Leveraging innovative technologies is crucial for addressing both immediate needs and planning for the future. Product owners should incorporate cutting-edge technologies into their roadmaps, such as smart grid solutions, renewable energy integration, and advanced analytics. This not only addresses current challenges but also positions the organization for future industry advancements.

In the utility sector, regulatory changes can significantly impact product development. Product owners need to ensure that their roadmaps align with existing regulations while also anticipating potential shifts. This involves proactive engagement with regulatory bodies and a strategic approach to compliance in both the short and long term.

Aligning the product roadmap with a long-term vision is critical. Product owners should define clear objectives for the future and ensure that each product initiative contributes to the overarching strategic goals. This alignment ensures that immediate needs are addressed within the context of a broader, forward-looking vision.

Regularly monitoring industry developments, gathering feedback from stakeholders, and assessing the effectiveness of product initiatives are vital. This continuous feedback loop allows product owners to refine their roadmaps, ensuring that they remain responsive to both immediate demands and future trends.

Product owners in the utility industry must adopt a strategic and adaptive approach to roadmapping. By understanding the industry landscape, collaborating with stakeholders, prioritizing based on impact, embracing flexibility, integrating technology, considering regulatory aspects, aligning with long-term vision, and maintaining a continuous feedback loop, product owners can successfully navigate the delicate balance between addressing immediate needs and planning for the future.

PART III: COLLABORATION AND LEADERSHIP

CROSS-FUNCTIONAL COLLABORATION: BRIDGING DISCIPLINES FOR SUCCESS

In the utility industry, effective product ownership requires collaboration across diverse disciplines, from development and engineering to marketing and regulatory affairs.

At the core of effective product ownership lies the synergy between solutions development and product owners. Product owners must collaborate closely with solutions developers to translate conceptual ideas into tangible, technically feasible solutions. Bridging the gap between creative ideation and practical implementation, this collaboration ensures that products not only meet the industry's evolving needs but are also robust and technologically sound.

The integration of Information Technology (IT) is integral to modern utility products. Collaborating with IT experts is vital for ensuring seamless connectivity, data security, and the incorporation of cutting-edge technologies. Product owners must work in tandem with IT teams to align the technological infrastructure with the overarching goals of the product and the organization.

Effectively bringing utility products to market requires a cohesive collaboration between product owners, marketing, and communications teams. Understanding consumer needs, market trends, and developing impactful messaging are crucial elements. Product owners should work closely with marketing professionals to create strategies that not only showcase the utility of the products but also resonate with the target audience. Navigating the regulatory landscape and ensuring compliance with legal frameworks are paramount in the utility sector. Collaborating with legal affairs professionals is crucial for product owners to understand and address regulatory requirements. This collaboration ensures that products are not only innovative but also adhere to legal standards, mitigating potential risks and fostering a culture of legal responsibility.

Cross-functional collaboration, while offering numerous advantages, comes with its own set of challenges. This chapter delves into strategies for overcoming these challenges, such as communication barriers, conflicting priorities, and differing timelines. It emphasizes the need for effective communication channels, fostering a shared understanding of goals, and establishing clear roles and responsibilities within cross-disciplinary teams.

Effective product ownership in the utility industry requires a harmonious blend of expertise from various disciplines. By fostering a culture of teamwork, understanding the unique contributions of each discipline, and addressing challenges head-on, product owners can lead interdisciplinary projects with finesse, ultimately contributing to the success of innovative and impactful utility products.

OVERCOMING CHALLENGES IN INTERDISCIPLINARY PROJECTS

Interdisciplinary projects in the realm of electric utility product development often encounter a host of challenges that can impede progress. Identifying and addressing these challenges is crucial for product owners to navigate complex projects successfully. Here, we explore common hurdles and practical solutions tailored to the specific context of electric utility products:

1. Communication Breakdowns:

Challenge: In interdisciplinary projects, communication

breakdowns between teams with different expertise can lead to misunderstandings and inefficiencies.

Solution: Establish clear communication channels and protocols. Regular cross-disciplinary meetings, project documentation, and the use of collaboration tools can enhance communication. Encourage open dialogue, ensuring that team members feel comfortable sharing insights and asking questions.

2. Conflicting Priorities:

Challenge: Teams from various disciplines may have conflicting priorities, leading to challenges in aligning goals and timelines.

Solution: Facilitate early collaboration and goal-setting sessions to align priorities. Establish a shared project vision and clear objectives. Regularly revisit and update priorities as the project progresses. Ensure that the overarching mission and strategic goals are well-communicated and understood across disciplines.

3. Differing Timelines:

Challenge: Different disciplines often work on different timelines, causing bottlenecks and delays in project completion.

Solution: Develop a comprehensive project timeline that accounts for the various phases and milestones across disciplines. Foster a culture of mutual understanding, where teams acknowledge and respect each other's timelines. Implement agile methodologies to allow for flexibility and adaptability to changing circumstances.

4. Technological Integration Challenges:

Challenge: Integrating diverse technologies can be complex, especially when different teams work on distinct aspects of the product.

Solution: Encourage interdisciplinary collaboration early in the project, allowing teams to understand the technological requirements of each component. Facilitate joint planning sessions to identify potential integration points and challenges. Regularly test and validate technological integrations to catch issues early in the development process.

5. Regulatory Compliance Issues:

Challenge: Ensuring compliance with evolving regulatory standards can be challenging, particularly when legal aspects are not integrated into the development process.

Solution: Involve legal affairs professionals from the outset of the project. Conduct thorough regulatory research and assessments at each development stage. Establish a clear process for legal reviews and approvals, ensuring that the product aligns with all relevant regulations.

6. Resistance to Change:

Challenge: Resistance to new methodologies or approaches from team members accustomed to working within their silos can hinder collaboration.

Solution: Foster a culture of openness to change. Provide training and resources to help teams adapt to new collaborative practices. Showcase the benefits of interdisciplinary collaboration through successful project examples. Encourage a mindset of continuous improvement.

7. Resource Allocation Issues:

Challenge: Competing demands for resources across disciplines can create resource allocation challenges.

Solution: Implement a centralized resource management system to transparently allocate and track resources. Clearly define resource needs at the project's outset and regularly reassess as project requirements evolve. Foster communication between discipline leads to optimize resource allocation.

By proactively addressing these challenges, product owners in the electric utility sector can enhance the effectiveness of interdisciplinary projects. Successful navigation of these hurdles not only ensures the timely and efficient development of electric utility products but also fosters a collaborative environment that harnesses the diverse expertise of interdisciplinary teams.

LEADERSHIP SKILLS: INSPIRING AND GUIDING TEAMS

Leadership is a cornerstone of effective product ownership. In this chapter, we delve into ten essential leadership skills that empower product owners to inspire and guide their teams toward shared goals, fostering a culture of innovation and excellence.

Visionary Thinking:

In the utility sector, where long-term planning and innovation are paramount, visionary thinking enables product owners to anticipate future trends and align product development strategies with the evolving needs of the industry.

Strategic Planning:

Given the complexity of the utility sector, strategic planning is essential for product owners to set clear objectives, prioritize initiatives, and ensure that product roadmaps align with the broader organizational goals and industry dynamics.

Effective Communication:

Clear and concise communication is vital in the utility space, where interdisciplinary collaboration is crucial. Product owners must effectively convey their vision, align teams, and articulate complex concepts to stakeholders, fostering a shared understanding across diverse disciplines.

Adaptability:

The utility industry is subject to rapid technological advancements and regulatory changes. Product owners need to adapt to evolving circumstances, whether in terms of technology integration, compliance, or market shifts.

Collaborative Leadership:

Collaboration is inherent in product ownership, especially in the utility sector where projects involve diverse teams. Collaborative leadership skills empower product owners to bring together experts from solutions development, engineering, IT, marketing, communications, and legal affairs, fostering a cohesive and high-performing team.

Decision-Making:

In a sector where decisions impact the reliability and sustainability of energy solutions, strong decision-making skills are crucial. Product owners must make informed choices considering technical feasibility, market trends, and regulatory implications.

Innovation Mindset:

Innovation is a driving force in the utility space. Product owners with an innovation mindset encourage their teams to think creatively, explore emerging technologies, and develop solutions that address current challenges while anticipating future needs.

Risk Management:

Risk is inherent in product development, particularly in an industry influenced by regulatory frameworks and technological complexities. Product owners must be adept at identifying, assessing, and mitigating risks to ensure the successful delivery of utility products.

Empathy:

Understanding the diverse needs of stakeholders, from end-users to regulatory bodies, requires empathy. Product owners who can empathize with the concerns and perspectives of various stakeholders can build stronger relationships and align products with broader societal goals.

Continuous Learning:

Given the rapid evolution of technologies and industry standards, continuous learning is essential. Product owners must stay informed about the latest advancements, industry trends, and regulatory changes to make informed decisions and drive innovation.

Leadership skills are pivotal for product owners in the utility sector to navigate the complexities of product development successfully. Visionary thinking, strategic planning, effective communication, adaptability, collaborative leadership, decision-making, innovation, risk management, empathy, and continuous learning collectively empower product owners to not only manage projects but to lead their teams towards creating innovative and impactful solutions that align with the goals of the utility industry.

PART IV: PRODUCT DEVELOPMENT AND DELIVERY

AGILE METHODOLOGIES: EMBRACING FLEXIBILITY AND ADAPTABILITY

In a rapidly changing industry like utilities, agility is key to successful product development. This chapter explores the implementation of agile methodologies, providing insights into adapting to changing requirements and fostering a dynamic environment that responds effectively to evolving needs.

Agile methodologies are iterative and flexible approaches to project management that prioritize adaptability, collaboration, and customer feedback. Unlike traditional, linear project management methods, agile methodologies emphasize continuous improvement, enabling teams to respond swiftly to changing requirements and market dynamics.

Key Principles of Agile Methodologies:

Iterative Development: Agile encourages incremental progress through short development cycles, allowing for frequent reassessment and adjustment of priorities.

Collaborative Teams: Cross-functional teams work closely throughout the development process, fostering open communication and shared ownership of project goals.

Customer Feedback: Regular feedback from end-users is incorporated into the development cycle, ensuring that the product aligns with user needs and expectations.

Adaptability: Agile methodologies embrace changes in requirements, welcoming them as opportunities for improvement rather than disruptions.

Application of Agile Methodologies in Utility Product

Development:

Rapid Prototyping and Testing:

Example: In the development of a new energy management software for utilities, agile methodologies allow product owners to rapidly create prototypes. These prototypes can be tested with utility operators, and feedback can be promptly incorporated into subsequent iterations, ensuring the final product meets the practical needs of end-users.

Continuous Feedback Loops:

Example: When developing a smart grid solution, agile practices facilitate ongoing communication with utility engineers. Regular feedback sessions allow the product team to adjust functionalities, address technical challenges, and optimize the solution in real-time, ensuring a more seamless integration into existing utility infrastructure.

Flexibility in Regulatory Compliance:

Example: Utility products must adhere to strict regulatory

standards. Agile methodologies enable product owners to respond swiftly to regulatory changes. For instance, if there are amendments to energy efficiency standards, the product development team can adjust the features and functionalities to align with the updated requirements.

Cross-Functional Collaboration:

Example: Agile methodologies foster collaboration between diverse teams, such as solutions development, engineering, IT, marketing, communications, and legal affairs. This ensures that all aspects of product development, including technological integration, marketing strategy, and legal compliance, are considered holistically.

Quick Adaptation to Market Trends:

Example: The utility industry is influenced by rapid shifts in market trends, such as the growing demand for renewable energy solutions. Agile methodologies empower product owners to quickly adapt product roadmaps to align with emerging trends, ensuring that utility products remain competitive and relevant.

Short Development Cycles:

Example: In the creation of a demand response application for utilities, short development cycles facilitated by agile methodologies allow the product team to release incremental features regularly. This approach ensures that utility operators can benefit from new functionalities without waiting for a lengthy development cycle to conclude.

Benefits of Agile Methodologies in Utility Product Development:

Faster Time-to-Market: Agile practices enable rapid development cycles, reducing time-to-market for utility products.

Enhanced Collaboration: Cross-functional teams collaborate seamlessly, breaking down silos and fostering a shared understanding of project goals.

Increased Adaptability: Agile methodologies empower product owners to respond promptly to changing industry dynamics, ensuring products remain relevant.

Continuous Improvement: The iterative nature of agile development allows for continuous improvement based on feedback and evolving requirements.

The application of agile methodologies in utility product development is instrumental in navigating the challenges of a rapidly changing industry. By embracing iterative approaches, encouraging collaboration, and prioritizing customer feedback, product owners can foster a dynamic environment that ensures their products meet the evolving needs and expectations of the utility sector.

RISK MANAGEMENT: SAFEGUARDING SUCCESS IN UTILITY PRODUCTS

In the intricate landscape of the utility industry, characterized by uncertainties and potential risks, effective product development hinges on a comprehensive approach to risk management. This chapter delves into the critical importance of risk management, offering strategies that empower product owners to identify, assess, and mitigate risks. These proactive measures are essential safeguards, ensuring the success and resilience of utility products in the face of industry complexities.

The Utility Industry's Inherent Risks:

The utility industry is inherently susceptible to a myriad of risks, spanning technological, regulatory, environmental, and market dynamics. From unforeseen regulatory changes impacting compliance requirements to the evolving landscape of energy technologies, product owners in this sector must navigate a complex terrain where uncertainties can manifest in various forms.

Importance of Risk Management in Utility Product Development:
Preserving Reliability and Safety:

In a sector where reliability and safety are paramount, risk management safeguards against potential threats that could compromise the performance and safety of utility products, such as grid management systems or energy storage solutions.

Compliance with Regulatory Standards:

Rapid changes in regulatory frameworks pose a continuous challenge. Effective risk management ensures that utility products align with evolving regulations, mitigating the legal and financial consequences of non-compliance.

Optimizing Resource Allocation:

Efficient resource allocation is crucial for successful product development. Risk management allows product owners to identify potential resource bottlenecks, enabling the optimization of resources to address and mitigate identified risks.

Enhancing Stakeholder Confidence:

Stakeholders, including utility operators, investors, and end-users, seek assurance in the reliability and success of utility products. Rigorous risk management builds confidence by demonstrating a proactive approach to addressing potential challenges.

Financial Viability:

Financial risks, such as budget overruns or unforeseen expenses, can jeopardize the viability of utility product development. A robust risk management strategy ensures that financial contingencies are considered and mitigated, safeguarding the project's fiscal health.

Strategies for Effective Risk Management in Utility Product Development:

Comprehensive Risk Identification:

Conduct thorough risk identification exercises at the outset of the project, involving cross-functional teams to capture a broad spectrum of potential risks. This includes technological, regulatory, market, and operational risks.

Risk Assessment and Prioritization:

Evaluate and prioritize identified risks based on their potential impact and likelihood of occurrence. This allows product owners to focus resources on addressing the most critical risks that could significantly impact the success of utility products.

Continuous Monitoring and Evaluation:

Establish a continuous monitoring system to track identified risks throughout the product development lifecycle. Regular evaluations ensure that the risk landscape is dynamic and responsive to changes in the industry or project dynamics.

Contingency Planning:

Develop contingency plans for high-priority risks. These plans should outline specific actions to be taken if a risk materializes, allowing for swift and effective responses to minimize the impact on product development.

Cross-Functional Collaboration:

Involve stakeholders from diverse disciplines, including legal, regulatory, engineering, and finance, in the risk management process. Collaborative efforts provide a holistic view of potential risks and enhance the effectiveness of risk mitigation strategies.

Scenario Analysis:

Conduct scenario analyses to anticipate and plan for a range of potential outcomes. By simulating various risk scenarios, product owners can better prepare for unexpected challenges and adapt strategies accordingly.

Regular Communication:

Foster open communication channels with stakeholders to keep them informed about identified risks and mitigation strategies. Transparent communication builds trust and ensures that stakeholders are well-prepared for potential challenges.

Risk management is not merely a precautionary measure but a proactive strategy to fortify utility product development against uncertainties. By systematically identifying, assessing, and mitigating risks, product owners in the utility sector can navigate the complexities of the industry with resilience, ensuring the successful delivery of products that meet the highest standards of reliability, safety, and regulatory compliance.

PART V: LESSONS LEARNED AND FUTURE TRENDS

KEY TAKEAWAYS FOR FUTURE SUCCESS

In reflecting on recent success stories in utility product launches, several key takeaways emerge, providing valuable lessons that transcend specific contexts. These insights serve as guiding principles for product owners, offering wisdom applicable to strategic planning, stakeholder engagement, and broader product development initiatives.

Embracing Energy Storage for Grid Stability:

Key Takeaway: The success of Tesla's Powerpack project underscores the pivotal role of energy storage solutions in enhancing grid stability. Product owners should recognize the importance of integrating energy storage technologies to address reliability challenges, support renewable energy integration, and contribute to overall grid resilience.

Data-Driven Optimization with APM Solutions:

Key Takeaway: ABB's Asset Performance Management (APM) solution highlights the power of data analytics and machine learning for optimizing asset performance. Product owners can leverage advanced analytics to enhance operational efficiency, reduce downtime, and extend the lifespan of critical assets, underscoring the value of data-driven decision-making in utility product development.

Advanced Grid Management with ADMS:

Key Takeaway: Siemens' Advanced Distribution Management System (ADMS) exemplifies the importance of advanced grid management. Product owners should prioritize technologies that enable real-time monitoring, control, and optimization of distribution networks. This approach enhances grid reliability, accommodates renewable energy integration, and positions utilities for future challenges.

Scalable Energy Storage Solutions:

Key Takeaway: General Electric's Reservoir Energy Storage System emphasizes the significance of scalable energy storage solutions. Product owners should seek flexibility and scalability in energy storage technologies to meet varying demands and support grid-scale applications. Scalability ensures adaptability to evolving energy needs and facilitates seamless integration into existing infrastructures.

Optimizing Distributed Energy Resources:

Key Takeaway: Duke Energy's Distributed Energy Resource Management System (DERMS) highlights the importance of efficiently managing distributed energy resources. Product owners should invest in systems that optimize the integration of diverse energy sources, including solar, storage, and demand response. This approach enhances grid flexibility, supports sustainability goals, and improves overall system efficiency.

Decentralized Virtual Power Plants:

Key Takeaway: Sonnen's Virtual Power Plant projects showcase the potential of decentralized energy resources. Product owners should explore the benefits of virtual power plants created by aggregating distributed energy storage systems. This approach contributes to grid stability, enables participation in grid services, and demonstrates the value of decentralized energy solutions in a collaborative ecosystem.

Guiding Principles for Product Owners:

Strategic Adoption of Energy Storage: Prioritize the strategic integration of energy storage solutions to enhance grid stability, reliability, and support the transition to renewable energy sources.

Harnessing the Power of Data: Embrace data-driven decision-making by leveraging advanced analytics and machine learning to optimize asset performance and operational efficiency.

Investing in Advanced Grid Management: Prioritize technologies that enable real-time monitoring, control, and optimization of distribution networks to enhance grid reliability and accommodate renewable energy integration.

Prioritizing Scalability in Energy Storage: Seek energy storage solutions that are scalable and flexible, allowing for adaptation to varying demands and seamless integration into existing infrastructures.

Efficient Management of Distributed Energy Resources: Invest in systems that efficiently manage distributed energy resources, optimizing their integration into the grid and improving overall system efficiency.

Exploring Decentralized Energy Solutions: Explore the potential of decentralized solutions, such as virtual power plants, to contribute to grid stability and provide opportunities for collaborative participation in grid services.

These key takeaways serve as guiding principles for

product owners navigating the complexities of utility product development. By embracing these lessons, product owners can craft strategic plans, engage stakeholders effectively, and drive initiatives that align with industry trends and contribute to the long-term success of utility products.

FUTURE TRENDS: NAVIGATING THE HORIZON

In the midst of the utility industry's rapid transformation, product owners find themselves at the forefront of navigating a dynamic landscape. To steer their initiatives toward success, it's crucial to not only comprehend the current state of affairs but also to anticipate and adapt to emerging trends that will shape the future of the utility sector.

Explore potential trajectories and identify key trends that are set to significantly influence product development and ownership in the years to come.

Integration of Decentralized Energy Resources:

The integration of decentralized energy resources, including solar, wind, and energy storage, is expected to continue its ascent. Utilities will increasingly focus on developing products and solutions that facilitate the seamless integration of these distributed resources into the grid. Virtual power plants and advanced grid management systems will play pivotal roles in orchestrating the diverse array of decentralized assets.

Continued Embrace of Renewable Energy:

The momentum toward renewable energy sources is set to persist, driven by environmental concerns and regulatory incentives. Product owners will need to align their strategies with the ongoing shift toward cleaner energy. This involves developing products that harness solar, wind, and other renewable sources, as well as storage solutions to mitigate intermittency challenges.

Grid Modernization and Smart Infrastructure:

Grid modernization initiatives and the development of smart infrastructure will shape the utility sector's future. Product owners will increasingly focus on creating intelligent solutions that enhance grid resilience, reliability, and efficiency. Smart grids, equipped with advanced sensors, communication networks, and data analytics, will become integral to product portfolios.

Electrification of Transportation:

The electrification of transportation is poised to have a profound impact on the utility industry. As electric vehicles (EVs) become more prevalent, product owners will explore opportunities to develop charging infrastructure and associated technologies. Smart charging solutions, integration with renewable energy sources, and grid-friendly EV charging strategies will be key areas of focus.

Advanced Metering Infrastructure and Data Analytics:

The deployment of Advanced Metering Infrastructure (AMI) coupled with robust data analytics capabilities will transform the way utilities interact with consumers. Product owners will need to develop solutions that leverage the wealth of data generated by smart meters, providing actionable insights for both utilities and end-users. This trend encompasses demand response, personalized energy management, and enhanced customer engagement.

Resilience and Cybersecurity:

The increasing digitization of the utility sector brings forth the imperative of ensuring resilience and cybersecurity. Product owners will need to embed robust cybersecurity measures in their solutions to protect critical infrastructure from cyber threats. Resilience planning, including the ability to withstand and recover from disruptions, will be a key consideration.

Artificial Intelligence (AI) and Machine Learning (ML) Integration:

The integration of Artificial Intelligence (AI) and Machine Learning (ML) will become more prevalent in utility product development. AI and ML technologies will enhance predictive maintenance, grid optimization, and decision-making processes. Product owners should explore ways to incorporate these technologies to unlock new efficiencies and capabilities.

Flexibility in Regulatory and Business Models:

The utility sector is witnessing a shift toward more flexible regulatory frameworks and business models. Product owners should anticipate and adapt to evolving regulatory landscapes, exploring innovative business models that align with changing market dynamics. This may include collaborations, performance-based incentives, and outcome-oriented approaches.

As the utility industry evolves, product owners must be adept at foreseeing and adapting to these emerging trends. The trajectory toward decentralized energy resources, continued emphasis on renewable energy, smart infrastructure, electrification of transportation, data analytics, resilience, AI/ML integration, and flexible business models will shape the future of utility product development and ownership. By aligning strategies with these trends, product owners can position themselves to be at the forefront of innovation and contribute to the sustainable and resilient future of the utility sector.

CONCLUSION: CHARTING A COURSE FOR STRATEGIC EXCELLENCE

In this exploration of utility product ownership, we've traversed the historical evolution of regulations, delved into successful product examples, dissected best practices, and anticipated future trajectories. The utility industry, ever-transformative, demands a nuanced approach from product owners who serve as the architects of innovation within this dynamic landscape.

Embarking on the journey of utility product ownership is an

invitation to become architects of change, innovators in a landscape defined by evolution. As we traverse the rich tapestry of historical regulations, successful case studies, and best practices, the call to action resounds with an urgency and opportunity to shape the future of the utility industry.

Seize the Wisdom of History:

In the annals of regulations, discover the foundation upon which the utility industry stands. Understand the historical evolution, appreciate the challenges overcome, and leverage the wisdom gained. Recognize that each regulation, each milestone, is a chapter that informs the next, creating a narrative that product owners now have the chance to craft.

The handbook of best practices is an indispensable compass for navigating the complexities of utility product ownership. As a product owner, embrace the strategic adoption of energy storage, foster cross-disciplinary collaboration, and implement agile methodologies. These best practices are not mere guidelines; they are beacons of guidance, illuminating the path toward resilient, innovative, and impactful product development.

Dive into the insightful case studies that unfold success stories in utility product launches. Extract lessons from Tesla's energy storage mastery, ABB's data-driven optimization, Siemens' grid management excellence, and more. Translate these insights into actionable strategies, for in the details of each case study lie the keys to unlocking innovation and navigating the ever-evolving utility landscape.

The future of utility product ownership beckons with emerging trends and trajectories. Anticipate the integration of decentralized energy resources, embrace the continued shift toward renewables, and harness the power of smart infrastructure and AI integration. Product owners are the visionaries who must not only foresee these trajectories but actively shape them, turning trends into transformative opportunities.

Now is the time to lead the charge for sustainable innovation. As a product owner, your role is pivotal in steering the utility industry toward a future that balances immediate needs with long-term planning. Champion sustainability, resilience, and customer-centric solutions. Embrace the responsibility to pioneer advancements that not only meet regulations but surpass them, setting new standards for utility product development.

Collaboration is the cornerstone of effective product ownership. Forge pathways of collaboration with diverse stakeholders—from engineering teams and regulatory experts to end-users and industry associations. The utility industry thrives on interconnected relationships, and as a product owner, your ability to navigate and foster collaboration is the catalyst for success.

In the dynamic realm of utility product ownership, the call to action is a clarion call for innovation, adaptation, and thriving amidst change. Embrace the challenges as opportunities, weave the wisdom of the past into the fabric of the future, and be the catalyst for transformative progress. The utility industry awaits the innovative spirit, strategic prowess, and collaborative energy that you, as a product owner, bring to the forefront.

Answer the call to action—shape the narrative, innovate boldly, and lead the charge for a future where utility product ownership is synonymous with sustainable, resilient, and groundbreaking advancements. The journey is yours to embark upon, and the time for transformative action is now.

ABOUT THE AUTHOR

Zachary Beaty, Mba, Pmp

Zachary Beaty is a seasoned professional hailing from North Carolina, bringing a wealth of experience in product development within the realm of regulated utilities. As a dedicated family man, USAF veteran, and accomplished project management professional, Zachary blends a robust foundation of military discipline with the strategic acumen honed through years in the corporate landscape.